A BOOM TO MANKIND

- ★ Blasts Hypocrisy
- ★ Explodes Chicanery
- ★ Bangs Indecency

Al Jaffee

BOMBS AGAIN

BY

Al Jaffee

A SIGNET BOOK

NEW AMERICAN LIBRARY

TIMES MIRROR

SIGNET, SIGNET CLASSICS, MENTOR, PLUME and
MERIDIAN BOOKS
are published by The New American Library, Inc.,
1301 Avenue of the Americas, New York, New York 10019

First Signet Printing, March, 1978

1 2 3 4 5 6 7 8 9

PRINTED IN THE UNITED STATES OF AMERICA

PREFACE

As my Uncle Carlo used to say, "Humor is no laughing matter." And for that matter neither was my Uncle Carlo. Aunt Sylvia, on the other hand (Aunt Sylvia was always on one hand or another—in fact, Uncle Carlo was fond of saying, "I can't seem to get Aunt Sylvia off my hands"), anyway, Aunt Sylvia certainly was a laughing matter. Several people were known to have actually died laughing at Aunt Sylvia. For a time there were serious discussions as to whether Aunt Sylvia ought to be declared a public menace. But instead, she was directed to wear a paper bag with eye holes and this simple solution seemed to satisfy everyone. Except, of course, Aunt Sylvia. She had a terrible time putting on makeup.

Their children, Frank and Ernest, were also unhappy. These fun-loving twins, who so much enjoyed starting the day laughing themselves into insensibility just from looking at their mother, now became wistful and dour. Which was a great improvement over Frank and Ernest. But after a while, Wistful and Dour forgot about their mother and formed a deep and abiding affection for the paper-bagged lady who fed and tucked them in at night.

Years later, while lying on twin therapy couches, Wistful and Dour experienced out their childhood traumas and soon found themselves becoming carefree and gay. Which was a great improvement over Wistful and Dour. Years of therapy had proved to Carefree and Gay that what they really missed in their childhood was not their mother's love but her unique ability to make them laugh. Yes, laughing was what it was all about, and now they surely knew it. They determined that henceforth they would laugh their way through life. No matter what the occasion. At happy things and sad ones. At bright things and dumb ones. At anything and everything.

It was with this in mind that the editors of this book decided to send a copy to Carefree and Gay for their earnest perusal and critical appraisal. Unfortunately, we cannot report their reaction because immediately after reading the book the twins were rushed to their shrink's emergency receiving room. It seems the book made them overwrought and depressed. Which is not as nice as Carefree and Gay. But then again, nothing is.

Signed,

Ziegelfeit Shtoonck
(which is a great
improvement over
Al Jaffee)

An uplifting
rocket story.

You can't
play with
this in
the house.

2

A touching collection of sentimental absurdities.

An earthy
garden tale.

MORE

MORE

A brave display of charming inanities.

A watered-down desert island event.

1

MORE

2

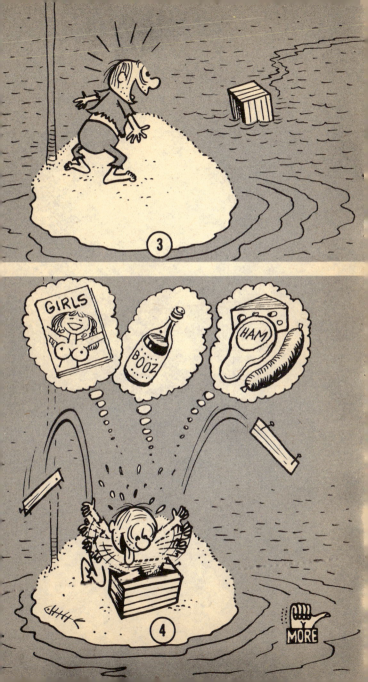

A forthright presentation of mild distractions.

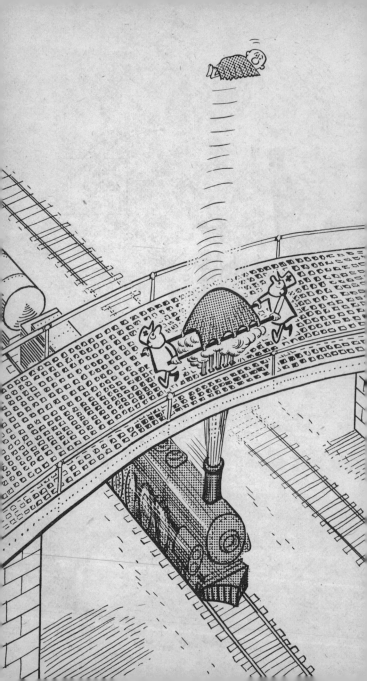

A strung-out
cat's cradle yarn.

NO . . . DON'T!

A solid aggregation
of stimulating nonentities.

A sticky painted park-bench thriller.

PARK

MORE

①

WET
PAINT

WET
PAINT

3

MORE

WET
PAINT

4

A fearless assemblage
of banal calamities.

SHOW
FOLK
HOTEL

PROF. ED
AND
CHARLY

A puffed-up smoke-signal farce.

①

MORE

②

3

MORE

MORE

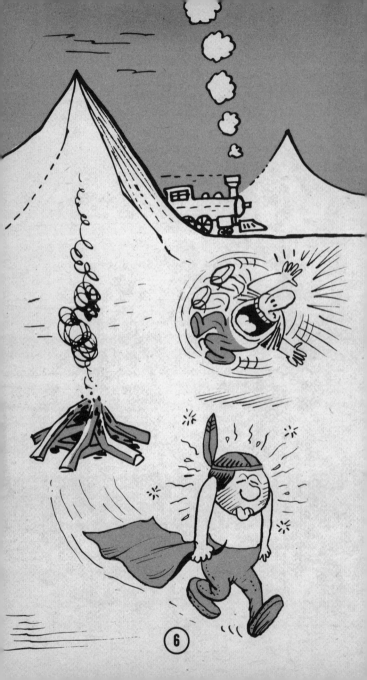

6

A courageous ingathering of bothersome nullities.

A pushy pushcart narrative.

① MORE

A heroic compilation of bland diversions.

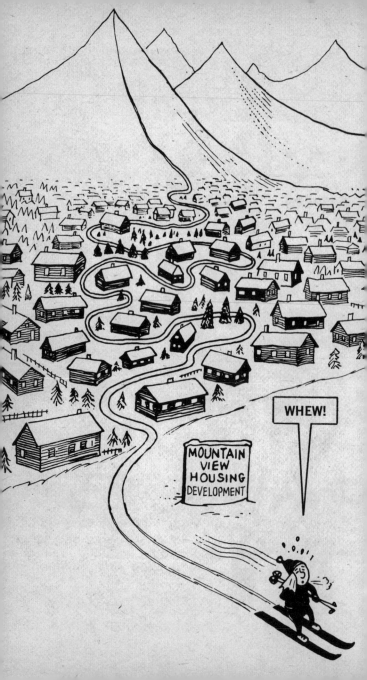

A bouncy trampoline epic.

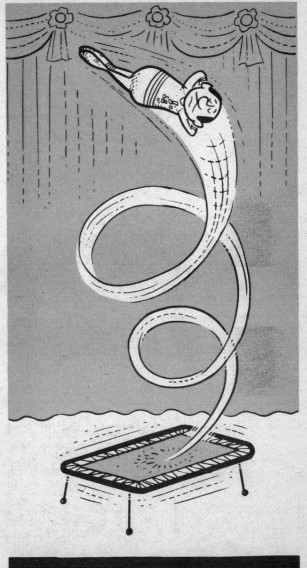

A plucky plethora of nostalgic nothingnesses.

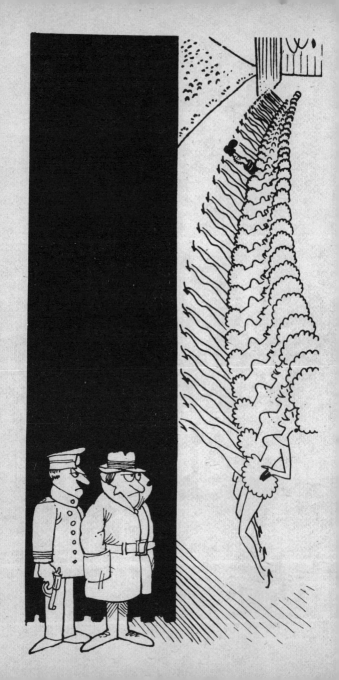

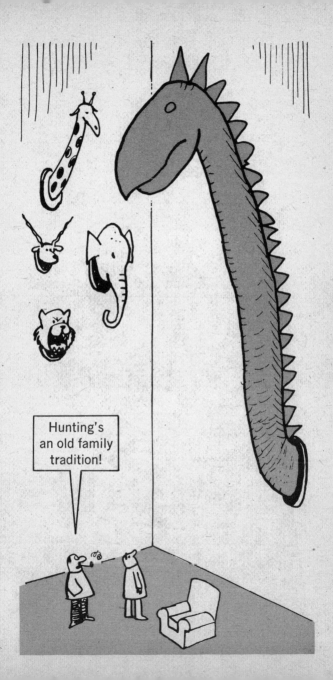

An out-of-left-field baseball saga.

MORE

③

MORE

4

5

MORE

⑥

A gutsy medley of lovable abnormalities.

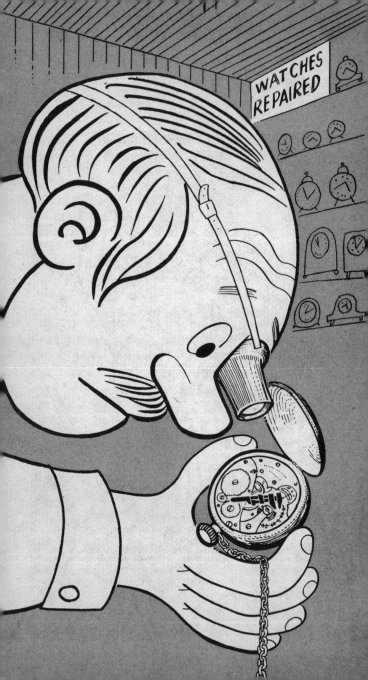

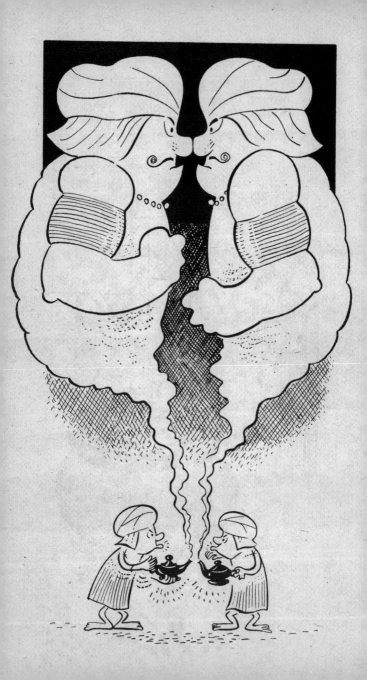

A questionable
information-desk diatribe.

INFORMATION

It's *that* way, Fred.

MORE

A defiant concoction of risible exasperations.

A prickly voodoo-doll episode.

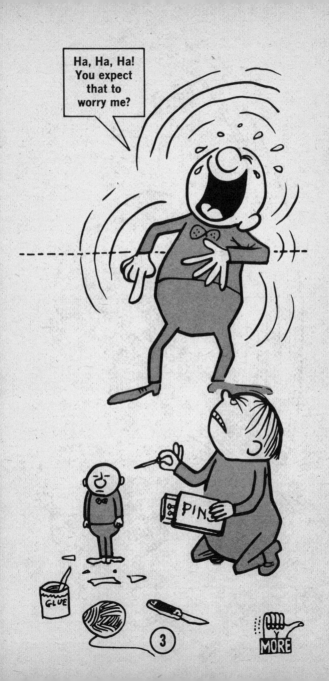

An intrepid cluster of delightful indignities.

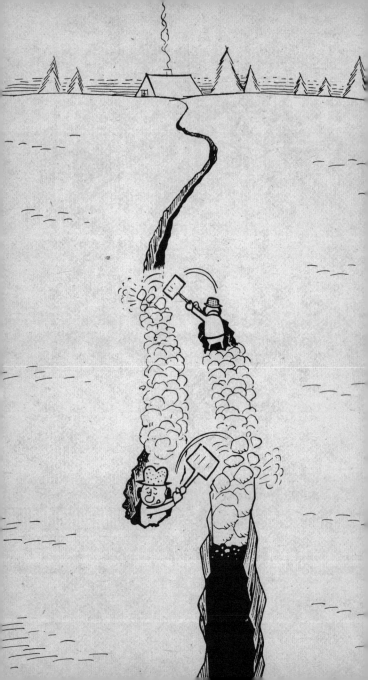

A half-baked
prison-cake adventure.

MORE

①

②

A stouthearted selection of ships and quips.

A punchy
prizefighting sojourn.

③

MORE

5

MORE

HURRY, HURRY, HURRY!
BUY THESE BOOKS!

Only 12,256,67~~8~~7 copies of these treasured classics left in stock.